Scottish Gaelic and its European Cousins

George McLennan

© George McLennan

First published by New Argyll Publishing 2022

For permission requests, please contact
www.newargyllpublishing.com

British Library Cataloguing-in-Publication Data.
A catalogue record for this book is available from the British Library.

ISBN 978-1-907165-44-3

CONTENTS

IN MEMORIAM

George Robert McLennan MA Hons, PhD 1945 – 2021

George studied the Classical Languages at Brechin High School, St Andrews and McMaster Universities and Birkbeck College, London, latterly concentrating on Ancient Greek, and also venturing into Sanskrit – and Gaelic – in London. He obtained three post-doctoral posts in the Universities of Bonn, Urbino and Nsukka, Nigeria.

George had met his wife Dorothy in St Andrews, in the Greek class, and she supported him in his journeys around the world. But they decided to come back to Scotland in 1975, and George spent a few years teaching in secondary schools in East Kilbride and Brechin. However he felt that his subjects were in decline and he and Dorothy decided that she should go back to her profession of librarian, while he took time to decide what he really wanted to do. Meanwhile he had taken the exam in Higher Gaelic and had expanded his knowledge of the language. This decision brought them to Argyll, where they stayed for the next 40-odd years.

He spent the time increasing his knowledge of Gaelic, reading and especially listening to the Gaelic radio programmes. He was part of the Workers Education Association team in the West of Scotland, and on tours of the country he was the 'Gaelic expert', explaining place names, which describe the terrain and use of the land. Additionally, he gave evening and afternoon talks and some Gaelic language lessons. It was his students who suggested that he should write this down, one of his students gave him a word processor to get him started and another had started a small publishing company.

He used the research skills learned working for his degrees as well as his interest in the history of languages to explore further and further into Gaelic and its place in the family of languages, always eager to show that Gaelic is not a strange outlier but has its place at the heart of Indo European languages.

Luckily for him, Dorothy had many of the same interests, with the basis of classical languages, so he was able to discuss ideas with her and share the pleasures of etymology.

George and Dorothy had two sons, Gregor and Euan, partners Ronee and Sarah, and three grandchildren.

Dorothy McLennan

PREFACE

The word *cousins* is used rather loosely in this title to indicate a close relationship between Gaelic and other European languages as well as a more distant relationship by adoption – for the latter see chapters 8, 9 and 10.

I have frequently used the form Irish/Gaelic as a shorthand way of indicating the development from Old Irish to present-day Gaelic. The latter is the main focus of attention, as the title of the book indicates, but many issues discussed are of considerable antiquity, which is where Old Irish comes in. Gaelic and its parent Irish were probably fairly similar for a few centuries after the language moved to Scotland around the fifth century AD, before Gaelic gradually found its own voice. Today it is regarded as a separate language in its own right, but references to Gaelic below can be assumed to include Irish, and vice versa, unless specified otherwise.

The Celtic language family is traditionally divided into two separate groups referred to as Gadhelic – also known as Goid(h)elic, and Brythonic – also known as Brittonic. Gadhelic includes Gaelic, Irish and Manx, while Brythonic includes Welsh, Breton and Cornish, the last dead by the end of the eighteenth century but now being revived by enthusiasts.

Russian and Greek words have been given in the Roman alphabet since some readers may not be familiar with the Cyrillic and Greek alphabets. Some other Slavonic languages, e.g. Polish use the Roman alphabet[1] but Russian is the most important Slavonic language by far. The tradition Irish Gaelic alphabet is no longer used in standard printing (books, newspapers etc.) but is still

---

[1] Polish adopted the Latin alphabet because it had become a Roman Catholic country and wanted to keep its distance from other Slav countries which were Orthodox and used the Cyrillic alphabet. Religion was also a factor in the Irish/Gaelic adoption of the Roman alphabet used throughout the Roman Empire and later where Latin was widely used.

found in place names, official signs and other conscious archaisms. It continued in general use up to the middle of the last century; it is based on the standard Roman alphabet, which it closely resembles, and although it contained the letter *h*, it used a dot placed above a letter to indicate lenition. Irish written in the modern alphabet uses *h* for this purpose, as mentioned below. This change to the new Irish alphabet bears a resemblance to the modernisation of the old-style German alphabet which changed to standard Roman script at around the same time. Scottish Gaelic, from the time of its first printed books in the 16th century, has never used the old Irish script.

When citing foreign words, especially Greek and Latin, I've tried to use those which are also found in English, as *omnibus*, which should help with further explanations.

I have only very briefly explained certain features of Gaelic such as lenition, the broad with broad spelling rule, the superlative and other points of grammar. These are adequately discussed in grammar books and other learners' material. Examples of cases of nouns refer to the fact that some languages, but not English, have different forms of a noun, with various endings showing that the noun is the subject, or object, or indirect object etc. of a sentence.

Finally, some of the features of Gaelic mentioned below are common aspects of the language today (e.g. the relative future in -*s*), while others are less common or obsolescent (e.g. the dative plural in **(a)ibh**). But because such features are, or were, found in other languages of Europe, they serve to show that Gaelic is not an obscure language quite unlike anything else, which is still a widespread misconception. Regarding individual words, I have occasionally mentioned cognates in other languages. A fuller account of Gaelic words and their relationship to English cognates can be found in *Gaelic and English – their common origins*, 2nd ed. New Argyll Publishing, 2018.

George McLennan

INTRODUCTION

In this book I've concentrated on the Indo-European languages of Europe rather than the many Indo-Iranian related languages, many of them descendants of Sanskrit. These latter are, of course, perfectly valid, but possibly, for present purposes, less interesting and certainly less familiar. There is a vast amount of material. According to the influential publication *Ethnologue* there are about 445 Indo-European languages. Most of these are not European, but are part of the Indo-Iranian section – Sanskrit and its numerous descendants, for instance – and there are apparently over 300 of these. A large amount of the 445 could be described as dialects and this often has to do with their perceived national status. A stricter definition of language as opposed to dialect would give around forty living Indo-European languages in Europe – any more are perhaps questionable. To what extent is Manx, for instance, (closely related to Gaelic) a living language? UNESCO now classifies it as 'critically endangered', having earlier described it as 'extinct'[2]. And is it maybe a variety of Gaelic?

Dialects are particularly strong in European countries which have been established only recently, Germany and Italy for example, though local dialects there have lost some of their status since unification. They can still be regarded as distinct languages, however. Sardo (Sardinian) for instance, is pretty incomprehensible to most other Italians. In contrast, Danish and Swedish are fairly close, mutually understandable, but are nevertheless regarded as different languages. Spoken Gaelic and modern Irish are fairly close, and with an effort you can usually get the gist, especially with Donegal Irish. But then some Irish speakers find the Irish of a different part of the country difficult, and the same used to be said of Gaelic (less so nowadays) and also of Scots. The Scots speech of

---

[2] Recent progress includes a Manx-medium primary school and Manx language radio broadcasts.

the north-east, mentioned below, would be regarded by some as a dialect within a dialect.

Another point mentioned below from time to time concerns Indo-European roots. These are the oldest and smallest units, usually one syllable and usually of three or four letters, from which all the native words in Indo-European languages are derived. These roots belong to what is usually called Proto-Indo-European, before it separated into the various language families which we have today (Celtic, Germanic, Slavonic, Romance etc.) and have been constructed backwards, so to speak, after an examination of cognate words in these language families. There are about 3000 such roots, which doesn't seem much given the vast amount of words in all Indo-European languages descended from them. But each root can be altered in various ways – the original vowel can change (e.g. from *e* to *o*) or disappear, an initial letter could be removed, and various suffixes of one or more letters could be added to form new stems.

One brief example involving a Gaelic word will illustrate how this is done. **Uisge** 'water' is from a Proto-Indo-European root *wed-. From the -*e*- grade of this root comes English *wet*; from an -*o*-grade comes English *water* and *wash*, and with the suffix -*a* we get *woda* (now *voda*) the Russian word for 'water' which was then extended to *vodka*. And from a nasalised form with -*n*- comes English <u>winter</u> (the wet season). The -*u*- grade has removed the initial *w*, which is a semi-vowel often referred to as a glide in Indo-European terminology; the suffix -*a* is added to the nasalised form giving *unda*, one of the Latin words for 'water', common in the derived Romance languages and in English <u>undulate</u>, <u>abound</u>, <u>abundant</u> etc., with the general idea of overflowing, from Norman French. There is also a -*u*- grade form with the suffix -*r*, giving *hydro*, from Greek *hudor* 'water'[3], and *otter*, the water animal – most other Indo-

---

[3] The initial h, called a rough breathing, was a common feature of Classical Greek words starting with a vowel; it still exists but is no longer sounded. A Greek *u* is traditionally represented by *y* in English borrowings.

European languages have a form with *u*, like Swedish *utter*. Gaelic **uisge** is also a -*u*- grade form with a suffix -*skio*. We don't now know what the original significances of many of these affixes were and some explanations are not universally accepted; the authoritative Oxford English Dictionary has doubts about *winter*, for instance.

The swirling melting pot of Indo-European roots is well illustrated by the other main Indo-European word for 'water' found in Latin and its descendants as *aqua*, with the secondary meaning of 'river'. This does not appear as a radical in the Celtic languages, yet it is found as a borrowing from Old Norse *a*, 'a river' in river names in the Highlands and Islands, as Lung<u>a</u> 'ship river', Lochranz<u>a</u> 'rowan river loch'. The shortening of Indo-European *hékʷeh*, Latin *aqua*, to Old Norse a is *a* feature of languages over time; Modern French *eau* 'water' is a good example here.

CHAPTER 1
NOUNS AND DATIVES

Modern Gaelic retains features of grammar which have long vanished from other Indo-European languages. One of these can be illustrated by the word *bus*. This word is now common throughout Europe and indeed much of the rest of the world. It is, of course, a shortened form of the Latin word *omnibus*, meaning 'for all', the dative/ablative plural case of *omnis* 'all', and was first coined in France in the 1820s to indicate that this modern form of transport was not a private vehicle, but a public one open to everyone. This reflects the fact that Latin was much more widely known than it is today, which also accounts for the facetious coinage of another form of transport, the tandem, a pun on the Latin word *tandem* 'at length'. This elongated bicycle for two persons, one behind the other, first appeared towards the end of the 19th century, and has also been used for horses and canoes. When the horse-drawn omnibus gave way to its motorised form, the term motor bus came into use. Its appearance in the amusing poem by A D Godley illustrates the same feature of modern Gaelic, where the letter b, the key element of this dative/ablative case, is preserved. The Indo-European endings in question were actually for four cases, the dative, ablative, locative and instrumental, which merged eventually into what is now referred to as the dative case in Gaelic. The *-bis* ending of some of these cases is probably what led to the Gaelic **-(a)ibh** form.

Godley, an Oxford scholar, wrote his little verse in 1914 to mark the appearance of the new-fangled motor bus in Oxford. The poem mixes English and Latin (Godley was a well-known classical scholar), showing all the cases of the Latin noun:-

What is this that roareth thus?
Can it be a motor bus?
Yes, the smell and hideous hum

Indicat motorem bum. ....
How shall creatures live like us

Cincti bis motoribus?
Domine, defende nos
Contra hos motores bos.

Line 6, *cincti bis motoribus*, (surrounded by motor buses) shows the
-ibus ending also found in *omnibus*[4], and this is the noun ending
which survives today in Gaelic.

In Gaelic the ending takes the form **-aibh** or **-ibh** depending
on the previous vowel (the spelling rule!). This form, an archaic
survival, remains in a few phrases, as **air beulaibh** 'in front of', **fo
gheasaibh** 'bewitched, under a spell' and **mar fhiachaibh**
'obligated, beholden to'. The modern plural ending **-an** is rarely
used with these words, i.e. **fo gheasan** is not heard, and it certainly
wouldn't sound right. It's a bit like English phrases such as *cometh the
hour, cometh the man*, and *fare thee well*, which use an archaic part of a
verb and pronoun, but are still in occasional use today, and remain
quite acceptable alongside the more modern form. **Air cùlaibh**
'behind' also still persists, though it's now more written rather than
spoken. Some Gaelic dictionaries give **beulaibh** as a singular,
nominative case, meaning 'front, foreside', but this looks like a back
formation from **air beulaibh**. 'Front' is expressed in Gaelic by
words such as **aghaidh, aodann** and **toiseach**, and in any case **-
aibh** is not a recognised suffix – and there are dozens of these –
used in the composition of Gaelic nouns.

This old dative plural form is also found in poetry and song. A
well-known example is

---

[4] Many, especially Americans, will be familiar with the phrase *e pluribus unum* (out
of many, one) a reference to the melting pot, a fusion of different nationalities and
cultures in the USA. It's a motto of the United States and appears on its coins.
Pluribus is the dative/ablative plural of *plus*.

Guma slàn do na fearaibh thèid thairis a' chuan,
'Good health to the men who'll go across the sea'

a song written in 1838 by Donald Campbell, the Kingussie bard, to commemorate the impending emigration to Australia of about 300 tenants of a nearby estate. The 'modern' dative plural is **fir**, but this wouldn't fit the metre or rhythm of the line, as anyone who knows the song will testify. But there are instances of such modernisation elsewhere. The Gaelic psalms have many **-(a)ibh** dative plurals, not surprisingly, given their age (17th century). So in the 23rd psalm – 'The Lord's my shepherd' – the words 'in pastures green' were rendered as **air cluainibh glas'** and 'within the paths of righteousness' as **air slighibh glan' na fireantachd**. A version of this psalm has appeared with **cluainean** and **slighean**, the modern plural forms; such changes will not appeal to traditionalists, but they fit the metre. This is a less important factor, though, when the psalms are sung in the traditional Gaelic way, where metrical precision is not a priority.

Gaelic proverbs, reflecting the wisdom of ages, are also a source of such forms, as **bean le rosgaibh rèidh** 'a woman with tranquil eyes' – apparently something to look for when choosing a wife. Likewise Gaelic songs, such as the traditional **Mo Nighean Donn Bhòidheach** 'My Pretty Brown-Haired Maiden' with the line

Sann tha mo rùn sna beanntaibh
'my love is amongst the hills'.

And **Eilean an Fhraoich** 'Isle of the Heather' by Murdo MacLeod, with

'N àm èirigh na grèine air a shlèibhtibh bidh ceò
'at the time of sunrise there will be mist on the hills'.

Songs such as these are frequently sung at the national and local mods, and are very familiar. They were written in the nineteenth century, however, and the old/traditional dative plurals in them

14

don't appear in modern songs. The pop group Runrig, for instance, never use them.

Book titles can also have these old datives, as **Guthan o na Beanntaibh** 'Voices from the Hills', a volume published in 1927 as part of the process of raising funds for An Comunn Gàidhealach. As might be expected there are lots of old dative **-(a)ibh** forms to be found here. But any new book published today would be very unlikely to have them.

An earlier Celtic language, Celtiberian, spoken in Spain but dying out in the first century AD, also had this dative plural (in the form *-ubos*), as surviving inscriptions show. But the survival in Gaelic of the **-(a)ibh** dative plural is surprising because of its use with prepositions. It was the increasing use of prepositions in Latin which hastened the decline of the dative, and indeed all cases of nouns. When Latin prepositions such as *cum* (with), *pro* (for), *ad* (to) and so on, began to be used with nouns, it was not necessary, particularly in Vulgar Latin, to keep the case endings, especially since these endings had been gradually falling off the end of words, and the use of prepositions made the meaning clearer. A parallel of sorts in modern English is the pronoun *whom*, the form used as an object and with prepositions; it's losing ground to the form *who*, particularly in colloquial speech. So Romance languages today (apart from Romanian) have only the one form of the noun, based on the old Latin stem. Thus French *pour moi* (for me) was earlier Latin *mihi*, to which the preposition *pro* – now *pour* – has been added. Modern Gaelic, however, is almost the opposite. As a rule these **-(a)ibh** datives are always preceded by a preposition and do not feature on their own without a preposition, and this has been the general – though not obligatory – rule from old Irish onwards. Thus we have in modern Gaelic **do na fearaibh** quoted above, and countless others. In modern poetry an instance would be **canabhas ri cranntaibh** 'Canvas sail to the masts' from **Eilean na h-Òige** 'Island of Youth' by Fr. Allan McDonald in praise of Eriskay where he was parish priest and died in 1905. These old datives would have had a slightly exotic flavour, and this is probably why they were sometimes wrongly used by poets who didn't understand their grammatical pedigree.

There is a fascinating example of this from Neil MacLeod in his poem **Brosnachadh na Gàidhlig** 'Giving Encouragement to Gaelic' where the second last verse ends

> **'S a' Ghàidhlig aosd' le maoin gun èis**
> **A' gleus bhur macaibh.**
> 'And venerable Gaelic with its unblemished riches
> Inspiring your sons'.

In fact the whole of the last line is slightly unusual in that the present participle of **gleus** is normally **a' gleusadh**, but the poet may be recalling a local dialect[5]. In any case the last line has to rhyme with the last line of all the other nine verses, three of which end (in English!) with Professor Blackie and two with Blackie. Had MacLeod written the more modern version **a' gleusadh bhur mic** it would have ruined both the rhythm and rhyme. He probably felt that **macaibh** was more classy, and so preferred it to the obvious alternative **balaich** 'young men', which would have given the same meaning, metre and rhyme, as well as being correct Gaelic. Poets tend to prefer the subtle to the straightforward.

Professor Blackie, for whom MacLeod wrote his poem, was John Stuart Blackie, who had been heavily involved in the establishment of a chair of Celtic at Edinburgh University in 1882. A very famous scholar, he was Professor of Greek at Edinburgh at the time, having earlier been Professor of Humanity (Latin) at Aberdeen. He had also become proficient in Gaelic, translating much poetry into English, and so was not really someone to whom you should write a poem with a misuse of **macaibh**, which is here

---

[5] Neil MacLeod was a distinguished popular poet from Glendale, Skye, though he spent most of his adult life in Edinburgh, where he died in 1913. Many of his poems are still well-known today. They were published in **Clàrsach an Doire**, and went through several editions/reprintings, the latest in 2010.

filling the role of the objective, or possibly the possessive/genitive case, but not the dative. However, as mentioned above, lots of other Gaelic poets did the same, probably not fully understanding the issue. It might have been more tactful also, since the poem is written in Gaelic, to have used the Gaelic form of Black(ie), **MacGilleDhuibh**, which in fact MacLeod uses to refer to Blackie in his poem **Am faigh a' Ghàidhlig bàs?** 'Will Gaelic die?'. When Professor Blackie died in 1895, Neil MacLeod wrote a short poem in his memory, this time with no dodgy datives. So a rule of sorts could be that if these dative plural forms appear without a preposition in front of them, they are not genuine forms.

In passing it should be mentioned that English also retains a dative case after a preposition, but with pronouns rather than nouns, since English has lost its noun case endings apart from the genitive singular. So with me, to them, from us, and not with I, to they, from we, though these latter forms are, or were, widely heard in some English dialects.

CHAPTER 2
NOUNS AND GENITIVES
THE ARTICLE

Another noun case in modern Gaelic provides a parallel with Latin, but is quite different from most of the other Indo-European languages of Europe. This is the genitive singular, also known as the possessive case. In Latin many masculine/neuter nouns had the ending -i in the genitive singular; this can be seen in well-known examples borrowed into English, as *a.d., anno domini*, in the year of the lord, and *e.g.* short for *exempli gratia*, for the sake of an example. This genitive singular ending in *-i* is also found in Romanian and Albanian where it also, like Gaelic, features in masculine plural nouns. Both Romanian and Albanian preserve archaic Indo-European language features, as, for instance, four or five different noun case endings.

The genitive singular form in modern Gaelic, however, is curious. It has moved from the end of a word, which is where it was in Ogham, into the word, so it is now usually the second last, or third last letter of the word. So we have **ainm a' bhàird** 'the name of the poet', from **bàrd**. It is not clear why this has happened with the letter **i** since Gaelic is elsewhere quite happy to keep other noun case endings at the end of the word, which is the normal practice in other European languages. This can be seen in **solas na gealaiche** 'the light of the moon', where **gealach** has a final **e** added; in addition, Gaelic has frequent plural **-(e)an** endings as well as the **-(a)ibh** dative plurals mentioned above. **Gealach** is a feminine noun, but it also has an **i** inserted to mark the genitive case. So Gaelic, in using this **i** genitive, has gone beyond Latin, which had restricted it to masculine or neuter nouns. The genitive singular of a large class of Latin feminine nouns (the first declension) had the case ending *-ae*, but this was *-ai* in earlier Latin with the *i* having been taken from the masculine noun form discussed above.

This may explain why Gaelic preserves an *i* in the genitive singular of many of its feminine nouns. This letter *i* has an effect on the sound of a consonant next to it, as grammar books will explain, (s, for instance, with an *i* has an English *sh* sound) but it wouldn't matter as far as the sound was concerned if the *i* came after or before the consonant, though if it were the former it would, of course, add an extra syllable.

So Gaelic genitive singulars go with Latin, but not with almost all the other Indo-European languages of Europe which derive from an -*s* ending, still visible in English *king's* (earlier *kinges*) and other members of the Germanic family, as well as Latin nouns of the third declension, and some classes of Greek nouns (both classical and modern). The Slavonic languages have dropped this final *s* and end their genitive singulars with a vowel.

In the Indo-European language family there seems to be a general progression, over millennia, with the gradual sequence of:
1) noun endings added to the noun stem to indicate the various cases, whether object, possessive, dative etc., then
2) the use of prepositions in addition to and along with the noun endings to make things clearer, then
3) the case endings disappearing, with only the prepositions left to convey the meaning.

This last stage is where the Romance languages (apart from Romanian) are now, and have been, in their colloquial spoken form for nearly two millennia. Gaelic is still at stage 2, but so are other language families in Europe, including rather surprisingly, English which preserves a trace of this. We can say *the man's house* where *man's* is the genitive/possessive case ending, or we can use the preposition *of*, and say *the house of the man*[6]. But we can't normally

---

[6] In English the *'s* ending is more colloquial than the *of* form; in German it's the other way – *das Haus von dem Mann* is now more colloquial than the literary *das Haus des Mannes*.

combine the two and say *the house of the man's*, though you can sometimes hear this in colloquial English.

Gaelic, too, can use prepositions with the genitive case, as do the Slavonic languages and German. Colloquial Gaelic sometimes avoids this and uses the dative instead, as is happening in colloquial German too. All of this is part of the very gradual falling out of use of the genitive case in Gaelic, e.g. in feminine nouns, after present participles, and the increasing use of **de** 'of', which takes the dative case. The correct forms are still heard, of course, and usually always written, but colloquially they are often disregarded, more in some areas (Lewis, for instance) than others. They are still almost obligatory, however, in certain set phrases, as **dol fodha na grèine (grian)** 'sunset', **deireadh na sgeòil (sgeul)** 'end of the story'. But the decline in use of the genitive case is possibly what lies behind a colloquial form of the comparison of adjectives, which traditionally use the feminine singular genitive form of the adjective. So, for instance, 'more certain' is sometimes rendered as **nas cinnteach** instead of the correct **nas cinntiche**. Most would regard the former as bad Gaelic and not to be encouraged, but the gradual intrusion of such features is how languages develop, change and simplify.

Learners of Gaelic in this country are sometimes surprised by the fact that the language has no indefinite article; there is no word in Gaelic for English *a* or *an*. So **duine** can mean *man* or *a man*. Russians would not be surprised by this, nor would any other Slavonic speakers nor those in the Baltic states of Latvia and Lithuania. But all the languages in the Romance and Germanic families have the indefinite article, with the curious exception of Icelandic. English might in fact seem rather cluttered to a Russian, since the major Slavonic languages (apart from Bulgarian and its neighbour North Macedonian) have no definite article (*the*) either! It is not clear why Gaelic didn't develop an indefinite article. It may be that it preserves an archaic linguistic feature; early Indo-European is thought to have had neither a definite or indefinite article, but some languages gradually acquired them. You can see this with Latin, which in normal usage had neither article; the Romance languages descended from it (Italian etc.) have both articles, having developed them from the Latin words for that (*ille/illa*) and one (*unus/una*). All the other Indo-European languages in Europe which have the indefinite article formed it from their word for the numeral one, as English *a* and *an*, variants of one. Gaelic could have done this; its word for *one*, **aon**, is cognate with all the other European numerals. But it didn't.

CHAPTER 3.
GENDER

Another similarity between nouns in Gaelic and other European languages, but a difference from English, concerns gender. This is no longer a feature of English[7], of course, but Gaelic has both masculine and feminine nouns (and used to have a third type, neuter). For adult learners of the language this can create problems with the definite article, case endings and adjective agreements, but the situation is the same, and sometimes worse, in Europe. Many languages. e.g. the Romance family, have two, but, like Gaelic, have left behind the third, the neuter (apart from Romanian), which was in their parent Latin. But the Slavonic and most Germanic languages have all three genders. The use of these can sometimes seem strange, as in the often-cited Gaelic **boireannach** 'woman', which is masculine, a feature found elsewhere in Europe: German *Mädchen* and Modern Greek *koritsi*, both meaning 'girl' are neuter, with diminutive suffixes. These three come from different Indo-European roots and so have no connection with each other.

But where there is a connection, to what extent does Gaelic retain the original gender of an Indo-European noun, in so far as we can deduce it from modern European languages? The evidence is conflicting. With a Gaelic word related to other European language families we can sometimes find conformity; Gaelic **olann** 'wool' is feminine, as is Latin *lana* (and hence the Romance languages), German *Wolle* and Polish *wełna*. These words are all from the one Indo-European root, which was therefore presumably feminine. But there are also examples of disagreement. The word

---

[7] You can, of course, say that the nouns *man* and *woman* are masculine and feminine respectively, but they are not treated grammatically in any different way from each other.

for *water* is a case in point. In Gaelic this is **uisge** which is cognate with Latin *unda* (hence English *undulate*) and German *Wasser*, Russian *voda* and Greek *hydor*. The Gaelic is masculine, the German and Greek neuter, and the Russian feminine. Or again **solas** 'light', which is masculine in Gaelic but its cognates are neuter in German, and feminine in Latin and the Romance languages; or **cridhe** 'heart', which is masculine in Gaelic, with cognates which are neuter in Latin and the Slavonic languages (Russian, Polish etc.) and feminine in Greek. In each case cognate words are all derived from the one Indo-European root, the stem tentatively reconstructed as **wed-* in the case of 'water', **lewk-* for 'light' and **kérd* for 'heart'. The English cognates for these words are, of course, 'water', 'light' and 'heart' respectively, but they do not have a gender; presumably in Old English/Anglo-Saxon they would have been as today's German.

All we can really say about this rather random attribution of gender is that it was already there in early Indo-European but its origins are obscure. Logic might suggest that words such as egg and milk would be feminine, but in fact they're certainly not feminine in the main Indo-European language families. Gaelic **ugh** 'egg' is masculine, as are the cognates in the Romance and Germanic languages, and neuter in the Slavonic languages. 'Milk' doesn't have a Gaelic cognate[8], but those in the Romance and Germanic languages are masculine, and those in the Slavonic languages are neuter. This can be rather bewildering, and it has to be said that Gaelic sometimes adds to the confusion, since a few nouns can be both masculine and feminine according to location. **Mìos** 'month' is a common example. In the rest of Europe (including Welsh) it's masculine, but it's both masculine and feminine in Gaelic and Irish. There are also instances in Gaelic where a word can have different genders according to its case: **talamh** 'earth' is masculine, but its genitive singular **talmhainn** 'of the earth' is feminine, and **muir** 'sea' can be both masculine and feminine, but its genitive **mara** is

---

[8] But one of the words for 'cow' **mart**, is masculine.

feminine. This sort of thing is not, of course, peculiar to Gaelic; many Latin and Greek nouns differ in gender between singular and plural of a noun. Some examples are Latin *caelum, rastrum, epulum, balneum* and *jocus*.

In passing, it's worth noting that modern nouns, i.e. those created in the 19th and 20th centuries, can be just as varied regarding gender. 'Radio', for instance, is masculine in Gaelic, feminine in French and neuter in German (as well as Romanian and Russian). 'A car' **càr** in Gaelic is masculine, but 'a van' **bhan** is feminine. Attempts to apply logic to all of this can provide some suggestions: most Latin words ending in *-io* (e.g. *legiō* 'a legion') are feminine, so French *radio* may follow this, and a 'v' sound at the beginning of a Gaelic noun indicates lenition, which is a feature of feminine nouns in the nominative singular. But there are many exceptions, such as **bhèato** 'veto', which is masculine.

CHAPTER 4.
ADJECTIVES AND ACCENTS

A more straightforward feature which Gaelic shares with other European languages, but not with English, concerns a noun with its adjective. In Gaelic this comes usually comes after its noun, unlike English which puts it before its noun. So Gaelic **taigh geal** is English *white house*. This is what might be called the default position, though there are exceptions; a few Gaelic adjectives always preceded their noun, as **deagh** 'good', **droch** 'bad'. The fact that these are exceptions is underlined by the fact that their Welsh cognates *da* and *drwg* come after their nouns. The Romance languages (French etc.) generally have their adjectives after the noun as a rule, but the Slavonic languages place them before. In all of these languages the change from the default position usually involves a slight change in the meaning of the adjective; an instance in Gaelic is **fìon dearg** 'red wine' and **dearg-amadan** 'utter idiot'. But all Indo-European languages in their earliest stages had a much more fluid order of adjective and noun and languages today reflect this. It might be thought that in languages which have different genders and cases, with which an adjective has to agree, it might be better if the noun came first so that the speaker would know how to treat the subsequent adjective. There is a certain logic to this, but it is not, in fact, what has always happened. The Germanic and Slavonic families mostly put the adjective before the noun, though German and Russian have three genders and are highly inflected. So broadly speaking you could say that in the placement of adjectives, Gaelic today goes with the Romance and Slavonic languages but not with English.

An unusual feature of adjectives in Gaelic (and Welsh) concerns their use to form adverbs. This is not done in the way that the other Indo-European languages of Europe frequently do it, by adding a suffix to the adjective: *-(i)ly* in English (as 'easy' » 'easily'), *-ment* in French, *-o* in Russian etc. Instead, Gaelic uses the preposition **gu** 'to' as a prefix to an adjective, as **gu trang**, 'busily'. This resembles one of the other ways which other European languages form an adverbial phrase – by using a preposition, as English 'with haste', 'in anger' and so on, but with a noun, not an adjective. Gaelic can do this too, of course, as **aig astar** 'at speed, speedily'. But its standard method is to prefix an adjective with **gu**, so it seems in principle that in Gaelic an adjective can also function as an adverb. This is an occasional feature of English too, as 'fast' (swift) which can be both an adjective and an adverb; there's no 'fastly'[9] or 'with fast'.

Still on adjectives, Irish shared the superlative ending meaning 'most' (*-est* in English 'biggest' etc.) with Latin and Italian *-issimus* or *-imus* (Italian *bellissima*, English *optimum* etc.). The *m* is the key letter. This feature has not survived into modern Gaelic, but is there in Welsh, as *talaf* 'tallest' from *tal* 'tall'. *F* is the standard mutation of *m* in Welsh, just as in Gaelic **mòr** » **mhòr**, and like Gaelic **mh**, Welsh *f* is pronounced like English *v*.

Another feature of Gaelic which is not found in English concerns the use of accents[10].

A wide variety of these, generally known as diacritical marks, occur in most other European languages – going back to the second century BC for Greek – so again English is the odd one out. The Gaelic accents are based on what was found in various Old Irish manuscripts, as with manuscripts in other languages, before the invention of printing. Gaelic, like Irish, now has just the one accent, a grave in the case of Gaelic, and an acute for Irish. These signify a long stressed vowel. Irish also used to place a dot above a

---

[9] Though it can be used as an adverb from 'fast' meaning 'tight, firm'.

[10] English occasionally uses accents, in poetry for instance, to indicate stress, as *learnèd*, or in a borrowed word, as *señor* 'mister'.

consonant as a diacritical mark to indicate lenition, but now, like Gaelic, uses the letter *h* for this purpose. Gaelic until recently used both a grave and acute accent to indicate the different sounds of the vowels *e* and *o*, which could help learners with pronunciation, but now there is only the grave. We're back to square one, as it were, since the translation of the New Testament in Gaelic in 1767, which largely established modern Gaelic spelling, used only the grave accent; in later editions the acute also appeared, but is now discouraged in Scotland.

Because written English does not use accents, editors of English language newspapers, magazines etc. – even in Scotland – frequently have a cavalier attitude to their use in any Gaelic words they may cite, omitting them more often than not. This is probably due to the fact that for many otherwise well-educated people Gaelic is still a bit of a mystery, so anything that looks roughly right will do; the spelling and grammar are also frequently not quite right. But many people have some acquaintance with French, so Scottish editors usually reproduce accented French words correctly.

As with other European languages, the accent on a Gaelic word also helps to distinguish between words otherwise spelled the same. There are quite a few of these, as **bas** 'palm of the hand' and **bàs** 'death', and they are all quite common. You occasionally find something similar in English with native and borrowed words, as *rose* (flower) and *rosé* (wine); unlike with Gaelic, editors will usually spell the latter correctly.

CHAPTER 5.
LENITION

The most difficult feature of Gaelic for learners is probably lenition at the beginning of a word. What this means is that some consonants change their sound under certain grammatical circumstances. This is such a basic component of the language that it appears from the beginning in grammar books and learners' material, so there is no need to illustrate it here. In modern Gaelic the letter h is placed immediately after a consonant to indicate lenition. It is interesting, however, to see how the Gaelic lenited consonants have parallels in European languages.

B, for instance, has a *v* sound when lenited (*bh*); a *b* in Modern Greek and Russian also has a *v* sound. Well-known also is the close similarity of *b* and *v* sounds in modern Spanish. In classical times a Greek *b* was just a *b* sound, so we have a gradual change over centuries. This is what happened in Irish too, as it moved away from earlier Indo-European. We don't know precisely when this happened, since the earliest manuscripts written in Irish (around the 10th century AD; earlier Irish manuscripts were of course written in Latin) sometimes have the dot above a consonant, as mentioned above, to illustrate lenition, so we can probably assume that lenition happened centuries earlier. The difference between *b* of Greek and Russian compared with the Gaelic *b* is, of course, that the first two have only one sound, while the Gaelic *b* has two.

C, which is always hard, like *k*, has a *ch* sound as in *loch* when lenited (*ch*). The transition from *lake* to *loch* shows this feature, as does English make with German *machen*. The Tuscan dialect of Italian has *la hasa* for *la casa* 'the house' which takes things a step further, the steps being c » ch » h. This is actually a common conversion between cognate Gaelic and English words, as **cù** and *hound*, **cridhe** and *heart* and so on.

D and *G* when lenited (*dh* and *gh*) before *e* or *i* have a sound somewhat similar to *y*, as in English *yes*; after *e* or *i* they are normally silent. *G* has parallels within Germanic, as German *gestern* and English *yesterday* and *gähnen* and *yawn*. The English words began with a *g* in Old English, so it has developed in a way that German has not, though in the case of *gate* and its variant *yett* (now chiefly Scots) it's the other way round – the *g* form is the more prominent today. There is also the standard English substitution of *y* for German *g* at the end of the word – *Tag* and *day* etc. Gaelic goes with German in this, as **minig** 'often, i.e. many times', cognate with English *many*, *manige* in earlier German, which survives in modern German *mannigfaltig* 'various, varied'. In borrowing words from English Gaelic uses **dh** or **gh** at the end of a word but treats them according to its own spelling conventions. Thus **bàgh** 'bay, creek' has the typical sound of a voiced **ch**, because it follows a broad vowel, whereas in **plòidh** 'ploy' the *dh* has a *y* sound.

F has no sound when lenited, that is, *fh* is silent. The reason for this may have something to do with the fact that *f* is the only Gaelic consonant which has not come from an earlier Indo-European consonant, as the other Gaelic consonants have. *F* has come from the Indo-European (semi)vowel *w*, sometimes described as a glide. Its sound is feeble enough to start with, and when it was lenited or softened it's not surprising that nothing remained. As usual, something similar happens elsewhere in Europe. An *h* at the start of a word is not pronounced now in Spanish, and many words in which this happens began with *f* in the parent Latin: so *hablar* 'to speak', Latin *fābulāre* (English *fable*), *hija* 'daughter', Latin *fīlia* (English *filial*) and so on. Why Spanish but none of the other Romance languages did this is not clear, but Basque, which didn't at first have an *f*, is regarded by some as a possible influence. In modern Irish, *f* is used to make the future tense active, as it was in earlier Gaelic, but it's pronounced *h*.[11] There may also be another Celtic connection: Celtiberian, mentioned above, spoken in the

---

[11] Confusingly (for learners) *f* in the future tense passive is pronounced *f*.

north of Spain until the first century AD, was a Q-Celtic language (unlike Galatian, which was P-Celtic) and so would have had similarities with Gaelic. A curious connection between f and w is also found in Scots, where the north east dialect substitutes initial f for $w(h)$ in interrogatives, mainly, but also in other words. So *wha* (who) is *fa*, *whit* (what) is *fit* and so on. Aberdeen is affectionately referred to by other Scots as furry boots (whereabouts) city.

M is treated like b with lenition (*mh*), i.e. it has the sound of v.[12] Both b and m are bilabials, and some Gaelic words which now begin with b earlier began with m, which was the Indo-European form. So **bleoghain** 'to milk' is cognate with English *milk*; **blas** 'taste' was earlier **mlas**, and has Slavonic cognates beginning with m. You can see this feature in the same word; **bean** 'woman. wife', has the plural **mnathan** (the *th* is there only to separate the vowels).

S when lenited (*sh*) has the sound of h. This interchange is common in Latin and Greek, represented in English borrowings such as s̲extet/h̲exagon, s̲eptet/h̲eptagon, s̲emi/h̲emi and so on. An older Indo-European instance gives the names Siegfried and Hector which come from the root *seg^h*, meaning 'champion, victor, defender'. And the Bavarian dialect of German has *han* for the standard *sind*.

T when lenited (*th*) also has the sound of h. Cognates in English and other European languages have the form *th*, as *three*, *thin* etc. Some Central Belt Scots pronounce words like *think* as *hink*, and *thing* like *hing*, but this is regarded as uneducated speech or slang. Yet words in English beginning with *wh* are regularly 'mispronounced' in England, where the h isn't sounded. In earlier English such words were written *hw-* and would have been pronounced as they are today in Scotland, Ireland and much of North America, with the h sounded. So there must have been a stage in England where what is now the current pronunciation was regarded as uneducated

---

[12] When lenited, it is sometimes sounded like English w, or even not sounded at all in some areas, but the usual sound is v.

and illiterate when it first appeared – yet it is now perfectly acceptable in England, if not elsewhere. Illiterate is not too strong a word if we consider the well-known Post Office issue (and hasty withdrawal) in 2007 of stamps featuring the Isle of White (sic) off southern England. And probably there is, or will be, a reference somewhere to Prince Charles as the Prince of Whales; given his interest in natural environment, fisheries etc. this could be more appropriate than a reference to a principality with which he has little affinity! Gaelic doesn't have the *wh* sound, but since all Gaelic speakers are now bilingual, you might expect the Scottish pronunciation to prevail. But a recent (2019) quiz programme in Gaelic on the BBC called the Isle of Wight *An t-Eilean Geal*, which is nonsense[13].

A few words about the letter *p*. An Indo-European *p* disappeared in early Celtic, though leaving a few modified traces here and there. So most Gaelic words beginning with *p* are borrowings. The absence of *p* is seen in words like **athair** 'father' alongside cognates such as *paternal, padre, père* etc. This missing *p*, however, is also a feature of Armenian, as *hur* 'fire', cognate with *pyre* (and *fire*), *hayr* 'father', cognate with **athair** above.

---

[13] Perhaps **Eilean Beichd** might do, based, like Welsh *Ynys Wyth*, on the Latin name *Vectis*, of uncertain meaning but widely used on the island, e.g. the Southern Vectis Bus Company. Gaelic translations of English placenames can be hilariously inaccurate sometimes, as, for example, Liverpool rendered as **Poll a' Ghrùthain**, where the last word refers to the liver of an animal. Liverpool probably means 'pool of muddy water', though there are other suggestions, but none of them have anything to do with the liver. Irish, with *Aepholl*, is even worse.

CHAPTER 6.
VERBS WITH S AND R
WORD ORDER

Another old grammatical feature retained in modern Gaelic is the future tense with *s*, which appears at the end of the verb. This is what grammar books call the relative future, because it's the form used in relative clauses and other occasions, and often found in proverbs, as **am fear a dh'iarra<u>s</u> smùirnean, gheibh e smùirnean**, 'the man who looks for a blemish will find it'. These futures can often be translated by a present tense in English, and this also applies to the normal, i.e. non-*s*, future as **saoilidh mi** 'I think'. Although the -*s* future is now restricted to relative clauses etc., it was actually the normal future tense in the north and east of the country, for instance in Sutherland, where Gaelic has now virtually vanished. It has a good claim to be the real future form since a future with *s* was one of the future tense forms in Old Irish. But because latterly it wasn't mainstream Gaelic, its use as a simple future was often viewed as an aberration of dialect.

Elsewhere in Europe the future tense was normally made with *s* in classical Greek. An illustration of this is the saying attributed to Archimedes, illustrating the power of leverage: 'Give me somewhere to stand and I will move the earth.' 'I will move' is *kineso* with the *s* added to the root *kineo* 'I move', borrowed by English as *cine-*, *cinema* (the <u>mov</u>ies). Early Latin also had an *s* future, but this didn't survive by the time of the Roman empire, and is not, of course, found in the Romance languages, which use their verb 'to have' as an auxiliary to create the future tense. And the long-dead Celtiberian language of northern Spain, mentioned above, had an *s* future. Modern Greek too has lost its s future. But Lithuanian makes the future tense by adding *s*, so both it and Gaelic preserve a feature lost elsewhere. Lithuanian often stands apart from other Indo-European languages of Europe; for instance, all of them (apart from Albanian) use the Indo-European root *séh₂ls* for 'salt', but Lithuanian has *druska*, with the sense of 'crumbs, fragments'.

Another feature of *s* in Gaelic with European parallels is the so-called moveable *s*, also known as a mobile or inorganic *s*. This is found at the beginning of a cognate word in some Indo-European languages but not in others. Its presence or absence seems arbitrary, but it is thought that it may reflect the ending of a previous word or perhaps the type of consonant immediately following the *s*. This *s* is missing in Gaelic **tarbh** 'bull', but not in its probable Germanic cognate, English *steer*. Conversely it is there in Gaelic **sneachd** 'snow' but not in Latin and the Romance languages cognate, French *neige*. There are lots of examples of this; the best known without the initial *s* is Gaelic **tha** 'am, is, are' the most common Gaelic verb. Cognates in Italian *sta*, Spanish *esta* and other Romance languages have the *s*, as does English *stand*. They are used of temporary situations, as Italian *come sta* 'how are you' (at the moment)? – **ciamar a tha thu?** This mobile *s* can feature even within the same language, as English *(s)quash*, or Gaelic **(s)màg**, also **smòg**, 'paw' in different dialects. The different Celtic languages also show both forms, as Gaelic **snàmh** 'swim', and Welsh *nawf*.

Gaelic's use of the passive voice[14] with *r* is another survival from early Indo-European. Latin used *r* in this way, as did two or three other obscure dead languages. A Latin instance, borrowed into English, is *imprimatur*, a 'go-ahead', or permission to do something. Its literal translation is 'let it be published', referring originally to a book allowed to be published by the Roman Catholic Church. The Romance languages do not make their passives in this way, but use their equivalent of the verb to be, as of course does English, as 'let it be published' above. The Germanic (but see Swedish and Danish below) and Slavonic languages do the same. Modern Greek continues to use its ancient verb endings for the passive.

---

[14] Example: 'I wrote this' is the active, 'this was written by me' is the passive.

But the Gaelic (and Welsh) passive with *r* is losing ground and is more literary than colloquial. Whereas Latin used it in the present, past, future etc., it is restricted to the future tense and the passive imperative in Gaelic and Welsh (the impersonal imperative). So **brisear an uinneag** 'the window will be broken', and Welsh *gwelir* 'it will be seen'. There are also impersonal verb forms in Gaelic ending in *r* and found in all tenses but these are literary rather than colloquial, and in any case the *r* is replaced by *s* in many districts. With this latter point it is interesting that Swedish and Danish make their passives, with which the impersonal has a certain affinity, by adding a final *s* to the verb.

But these forms of passive are felt as literary. In colloquial speech Gaelic follows other European languages in using an auxiliary verb to make the passive, as English does with the verb 'to be'. So **bidh an taigh air a leagail** 'the house will be demolished'. The most common way in Gaelic, however, is to use the verb **rach** 'to go' as an auxiliary, as **chaidh am bàta a thogail** 'the boat was built'. The idea of movement or progress involved in forming the passive can be seen also in the Italian (and other minor Italic languages such as Ladin, Romansh etc.) use of *venire* 'to come': *la barca venne costruita* 'the boat was built'. Another Celtic language, Welsh, uses *cael* 'to get' in the same way, something which is also found in colloquial, informal English: 'she got sent home', *cafodd hi ei hanfon adref*.

Another curious feature of Gaelic which sets it apart from English and other languages is the fact that the verb is usually the first word in a sentence or clause, as **chunnaic am balach an cù**, 'the boy saw the dog'. Certain words such as conjunctions, negatives, interrogatives etc. can sometimes precede the verb, as **cò chunnaic an cù?** 'who saw the dog?'. But the standard pattern is verb + subject + object. This order can sometimes be found in English poetry, for metrical reasons or to give an archaic flavour, but starting a sentence with the main verb (as opposed to an auxiliary) is not done. In Spanish, however, it is found occasionally and is perfectly acceptable; Modern Greek too can put the verb first, as did classical Greek and Latin from time to time. The picture is complicated, however, with these ancient languages, since the examples we have are from poetry and formal prose – the speeches of Cicero, for instance – and do not always reflect everyday common speech. There are also instances in old Welsh poetry of the subject coming before the verb, but in colloquial common speech Welsh is the same as Gaelic. There is evidence, however, that early Indo-European may have put the verb first in some of its language families, as happens in Gaelic. So again we have Gaelic retaining an old feature of language which has vanished from most of the rest of Europe.

Languages like Gaelic, which begin a sentence with a verb, have the subject immediately after it. Gaelic's use of **mi** as the subject pronoun (English *I*) is very unusual. This form with *m* is the accusative (objective) case in Proto-Indo-European, and becomes the objective forms in the later languages – as English *me*, Russian *menya* etc. – and Gaelic too, which means that **mi** can mean both 'I' and 'me'. Why Celtic languages used the Indo-European objective form and ignored the subject form is not clear; the latter was, of course, there in Proto-Indo-European as **éǵh₂* (or similar), which became *ego* in Latin, *ich* in German, *I* in English and so on. But there may be a connection with the first person verb ending *-mi* found in some old languages such as Sanskrit and Greek and so also in Proto-Indo-European. So Classical Greek has *didomi* 'I give', but the *-mi* ending has dropped off in Modern Greek, and 'I give' is now *dino*. But modern Greek retains from classical times the similar first person ending *-mai*, as *erchomai* 'I come', *eimai* 'I am'. In general, there is a feeling that the letter *m* is often associated with the first person ending of verbs; English *I am*, Latin *sum* etc. It's much the same in the Baltic (Latvian etc.) and Slavonic languages (e.g. Polish *jestem Szkotem* 'I'm Scottish'). The main difference on paper with Gaelic is that the pronoun isn't joined to the verb. In any case there is no uniformity in Europe with pronouns. The Romance languages do not distinguish between 'we' and 'us' (all from Latin *nos*, itself originally meaning 'us'), nor do the Celtic ones (Gaelic **sinn**), but the Slavonic languages do – Polish *my* 'we' and *nas* 'us'.

It should be pointed out that that in Gaelic there isn't really any confusion about whether **mi** is the subject or object in a sentence, since 1) the word order, mentioned above, clarifies matters; so **chunnaic mi e** 'I saw him', but **chunnaic e mi** 'he saw me'. And 2) the object pronoun is frequently combined with a preposition as one word, in a situation where English would often simply use the direct object. So **dh'fhaighnich mi dhi** 'I asked her', where **dhi** is a combination of **de** 'of' and **i** 'her'. Most Gaelic prepositions are combined with the personal pronouns in a similar way, and grammar books provide full lists. This is a feature of Gaelic which is not found in the other Indo-European languages of Europe, and for learners it takes a bit of getting used to.

CHAPTER 7.
NUMERALS.

The traditional Gaelic system of counting is another feature which is slightly different from English, but similar to the Romance and Slavonic languages. In English and the other Germanic languages the teens start at thirteen, whereas in Gaelic they start at eleven, as they do in French and Russian, say. So Gaelic **aon deug** 'eleven' (literally 'one ten'). But in fact the origin of English 'eleven' and 'twelve' reveal an underlying decimal system, as in Gaelic. 'Eleven' is the modern form of Old Germanic *ainlif* 'one left' i.e. one left over – the most likely explanation – after ten, so eleven in total. Similarly 'twelve' is *twalif*, two left over (after ten). So it's a decimal system of sorts, though the word ten doesn't make an appearance until 'thirteen'. In Lithuanian the word for ten doesn't appear at all, and it follows the old Germanic pattern up to nineteen. Lithuanian is a language which retains many Indo-European features which have now vanished from other European languages.

Gaelic's use of numerals is in fact quite straightforward compared with its fellow Celtic language Welsh. In the traditional Welsh 20s system sixteen is 'one on fifteen' *un ar bymtheg*, eighteen is 'two nines' *deunaw*, and nineteen is 'four on fifteen' *pedwar ar bymtheg*. Modern Breton has, not surprisingly, simplified this, except for eighteen, which is 'three sixes', though there is now also a more 'normal' form. And Welsh has now adopted a decimal system, so eleven is *un deg un* (one ten followed by one) and so on, though the traditional method is still used to tell the time and in naming years.

Gaelic differs from most other European languages also in its traditional system of counting in 20s. This is the norm in Danish, and there are instances in English, French and Albanian, but it is otherwise a feature of the Celtic languages[15]. But they too are now

---

[15] But it wasn't the original method in Old and Middle Irish, which used the 'ten' forms for 20 to 90. So the current 'new' way of counting could be regarded as a back

conforming to the normal European decimal pattern which, in the case of Gaelic, will probably eventually become the norm. At the moment, broadly speaking, the younger generation use the decimal system but the older generation usually don't as it wasn't commonly heard fifty years ago, say. The latter often simply use English numerals, since traditional counting in Gaelic can involve mental dexterity which many would rather avoid if possible. The year 1745 for instance is **seachd ceud deug dà fhichead 's a còig** (seven hundred ten two twenties and five) in traditional counting. The more traditional alternative **Bliadhna Theàrlaich** (Charlie's Year) cuts the Gordian knot in this instance! Modern Welsh has got round this rather well by simply saying each number by itself; 1745 is rendered as 'one seven four five' *un saith pedwar pump*. Gaelic, following English, does this with road numbers, e.g. the A947, but not with years.

The Gaelic use of the numeral 'two' **dà** is another example of its difference from English, but similarity to some other European languages. **Dà** doesn't take a plural form of a noun; so **aon leabhar**, **dà leabhar**, then **trì leabhraichean**. But English 'one book', 'two books' etc.

The reason for this is that in Old Irish nouns had three numbers – singular, dual, and plural – and the dual was used with nouns which came in pairs, as 'hands', 'feet', 'eyes' etc. and then anything with **dà** in front of it. In modern Gaelic **dà** is followed by the dative singular, so there would be a slight change if the noun is feminine, and no change if it's masculine. Proto-Indo-European had dual forms but these have now vanished from virtually all modern Indo-European languages. They are still there, however, in Lithuanian (obsolescent), and Slovene (still going strong). There are traces of this in English too with words like 'both', 'neither' etc.

---

to basics step. The 20s system is thought to have evolved from the use of 'twenty' **fichead** in multiplication, something still commonly heard today: 180, for instance, is frequently given as **naoi fichead** (nine twenties).

which refer to two persons/things, but it has long vanished from nouns in the Germanic family.

CHAPTER 8.
IRISH/GAELIC ON ITS OWN

Since there are instances where all the Indo-European languages agree with each other in having words from the same original root – the numerals 2 to 10, 100 and occasional words, as 'fingernail', Gaelic **ionga** (apart from Albanian) for example – it should be stressed that the opposite situation also occurs frequently. Very often a Gaelic word will be quite different from, and quite unconnected with, a word of the same meaning in other Indo-European languages. An example would be **sgàthan** 'a mirror' from **sgàth** 'a shade, shadow'; **sgàth** has cognates in many other Indo-European languages, but no modern Indo-European language uses it as the basis for 'mirror'. A suggested connection with Gothic (4th century AD) is uncertain, and this meaning has not survived in modern Germanic languages. See also Chapter 10.

The standard explanation for all this is that with a feature represented by the English word 'water' for example, the parent Indo-European language had different words for still water (lochs etc.), running water (rivers etc.), rainwater, drinking water, shallow water and so on. The various Indo-European language families then eventually settled on one of these options as their general word for fresh water. So Gaelic **uisge** relates to an Indo-European root with a general meaning of 'wet'; the Romance languages (Latin *aqua* » English *aqueduct* etc.) relate to an Indo-European root with a reference to running, swift flowing water. Another Celtic water word, Welsh *dŵr* is from a root with the meaning 'deep', or 'dark water'.

The moon and the sun also illustrate this point. Gaelic **gealach** 'moon' has a colour reference (yellow, white) whereas English 'moon' is from a different Indo-European root seen in the related word 'month' referring to a measurement of the time taken by the moon to revolve round the earth. Gaelic also had **luan**, but this was borrowed from Latin, used poetically and long obsolete as 'moon', but found today in **Diluain** 'Mo(o)nday', cognate with English 'lunar' etc. For **grian** 'sun' see below.

It is likely that all the Indo-European languages would have kept words in common for a considerable time before one or two gained the upper hand in a language family and the others fell out of everyday use, though sometimes retained in a different context, in place names for instance. There are instances of this Gaelic, of course. An example would be the word **ail** or **all** 'rock, crag' now obsolete, but retained in **mac-(t)alla** 'echo', and **All Chluaidh** (or similar in early Welsh), an early name for Dumbarton Rock, an old British stronghold on the river Clyde (Gaelic **Cluaidh**). **Ail** is probably cognate with English 'fell' (rocky hill) frequent in placenames as Goatfell, Campsie Fells etc., and with German *Fels*, as Drachenfels 'dragon's rock', a couple of well-known hills in Germany.

There are faint echoes of some of this in the Gaelic of today, though the picture is distorted by the overbearing effect of English on minority languages. Lewis Gaelic has come to make a clear distinction between running water, drinking water etc. (**bùrn** – borrowed from Scots) and rain (**uisge**). Gaelic speakers elsewhere generally don't have this distinction now[16], but use **uisge** for water in general, rain etc. though of course they are aware of the word **bùrn**; Fr Allan McDonald records its use – **bùrn chasa goileach** – for boiling water in South Uist[17]. But today it is widely regarded as a Lewis word, though why it has come to replace, in part, **uisge**, which must have been in general use in Lewis earlier, is not clear. But many Gaelic speakers outwith Lewis have long regarded imports from English or Scots as being an enthusiasm of Lewis Gaelic.

---

[16] But **bùrn** was apparently used in eastern Gaelic dialects where the language has now mostly gone.

[17] Gaelic Words and Expressions from South Uist and Eriskay.

However, many words in modern Irish/Gaelic don't seem to have cognates in other Indo-European languages of Europe. It is difficult to be certain in many cases why this should be, but an obvious possibility is that a word has been borrowed from a non-Indo-European language, or may even have a cognate in another long-lost Celtic language. Some of these non-Indo-European languages, such as Finnish and Hungarian, are still going strong today, and there would have been others in existence many millennia ago but now long vanished without trace. Italy, for instance, once had a few non-Indo-European languages (Etruscan etc.) and a well-established literary interest even 2500 years ago in such matters, but to the north – Scandinavia, and east – Russia, there is very little detailed information, apart from Greece. We are probably talking about hundreds of pre-Indo-European languages in Europe. As usual, it depends on what you mean by Europe – how far east can you go – and what you mean by language as opposed to dialect. Other Indo-European languages of Europe have words of unknown origin which are not Indo-European but belong to, and were borrowed from, languages spoken earlier but long vanished. A well-known example is classical Greek *thalassa/thalatta* 'sea', still in use today; and other often-cited examples are *perro* and *cerdo*, the Spanish words for 'dog' and 'pig' which have no convincing cognates in Europe although there is no shortage of suggestions (Basque, Celtiberian?)[18]. Regarding lost Celtic languages, some evidence may still turn up. The famous Botorrita bronze plaques of north-eastern Spain, with a wealth of Celtiberian inscriptions, date from the 1st century BC but were not discovered until the 1970s.

Some Gaelic examples are found only in the Gadhelic branch and not in the Brythonic family of Welsh, Breton and Cornish. It is unusual, however, to find a Gaelic word with no apparent Irish connection in this category, as is the case with **seillean** 'a bee'.

---

[18] Spanish also has the less commonly used *can* for 'dog', with cognates in the Celtic, Germanic and Romance language families.

The Irish word is **beach**, also found in Gaelic, though **seillean** is more common. **Beach** is an Indo-European word, with widespread cognates, including English *bee*. The absence of **seillean** in Irish – though it's in Manx – suggests either that it was there earlier but fell out of use, while retained in Gaelic, or Gaelic picked the word up from a pre-Celtic language in Scotland. If the latter, **seillean** would be later than the fifth century AD, roughly the time when Irish speakers moved to Dalriada in western Scotland and eventually began to develop their own form of Irish, leading to today's Scottish Gaelic. A common instance of this is a Gaelic word such as **dail** 'dale, meadow' which is ubiquitous in Scottish placenames (Dalwhinnie, Dalkeith etc.) but not found in Ireland. Gaelic presumably borrowed it from Brythonic (modern Welsh *dôl*) or Old Norse (*dalr*).

Here are a few Irish/Gaelic words which do not seem to have a cognate in other languages families of Europe. Most of them are actually fairly common words, which is not surprising since words in common everyday use by an indigenous people are more likely have influenced incomers.

Adharc – horn (of cattle etc.). No Indo-European cognate but a perhaps Gaulish or Basque connection.

Bagairt – threat.

Bathais – forehead.

Braon – a drop.

Craobh – tree.

Cron – harm.

Cùbhraidh – fragrant.

Feòil – flesh.

Gaoth – the wind.

Geur – sharp.

Giuthas – fir.

Gluais – to move.

Gruag – hair of the head.

Iasad – a loan.

Lach – wild duck.

Làidir – strong.

Lot – a wound.

Mèirleach – thief.

Meur – a finger.

Mullach – top.

Nàire – shame. A possible connection has been made with a Hittite word meaning 'reverence, modesty', but again no convincing cognate in the other Indo-European languages of Europe.

Oidhche – night. This is a good example of Irish/Gaelic using a word not used elsewhere. All the other Indo-European languages of Europe use the root *nók*ʷt or similar, hence English 'night, nocturnal' etc. So Welsh *nos* goes with the rest of Europe and not with the Q-Celtic languages. Gaelic however, still has the Indo-European root in *a-nochd* 'tonight' but has apparently borrowed **oidhche** from a non-Indo-European source.

Òrdag – thumb, big toe. Gaelic uses the same word for both, though 'hand' (**làmh**) or 'foot' (**cas**) can be added if necessary. The word is thought to be related to **òrd** 'a hammer', found also in

Welsh and Breton. but the etymology is quite uncertain. The root doesn't appear in any other IE languages.

Sgòrnan – throat.

Sionnach – a fox. This entry here assumes that there is no Indo-European connection and that apparent similarities are folk etymology. *Sion* or *sian* is an old Irish word for foxglove, and in modern Welsh it's *ffion* with typical Welsh initial *ff* equating to Gaelic *s* in words of Indo-European origin; the Latin cognate is *spionia*, a rare word used to describe a type of vine. The missing *p* is of course quite normal for Irish/Gaelic. What a fox has to do with any of this is unclear, and the usual suggestion is that foxglove is a corruption of folks' glove, the folk being the little people, fairies. This is in fact what the modern Gaelic means: **lus nam ban-sìth** 'fairy flower'. And yet the Welsh continue the canine connection with *bysedd y cŵn* 'dogs' fingers', one of their words for foxglove.

Sluasaid – a shovel.

Soitheach – a dish, (sailing)vessel.

These then are words which appear to be lacking cognates in not only other Indo-European languages but more specifically in the Brythonic branch of Celtic. There has, of course, been no shortage of suggested etymologies but none have gained general acceptance. You get the feeling, looking at the numerous suggestions of about a century ago, that there was a determination to find somehow an Indo-European cognate for most, if not all, Celtic words. But things have moved on, and many earlier etymologies are now regarded as unlikely. So the general feeling now is that words such as those just listed are just as likely to have been borrowed from an indigenous non-Indo-European language. In the case of Irish/Gaelic one possible source would have been whatever was spoken in Ireland at the time. The absence of cognate words in Welsh suggests that the indigenous pre-Celtic languages in Britain were unrelated to those of Ireland. The Celtic languages also picked up words from non-Indo-European languages on the mainland of Europe before they arrived in Britain, to judge from the few non-Indo-European cognates of Celtic languages found in branches of continental Celtic. So we may have a tantalising glimpse of ancient Ireland, but we also have to consider the possibility that some (or even all) of the above words which are apparently unique to Gaelic might have been picked up on the continent, since the fact that some continental Celtic (Celtiberian) were Q-Celtic, like Irish/Gaelic, and so a form of early Irish might have started life on the continent. At the moment evidence relating to the above list of words is lacking, but there remains the possibility of new discoveries, like the Botorrita bronze plaques mentioned above; or even a 'new' language such as Tocharian, once spoken in north east China, but long dead, the most easterly Indo-European language. Manuscripts in its distinctive alphabet were discovered in the 20th century.

Another theory is that non-Celtic Indo-European speakers had arrived in Britain and Ireland before the later Celtic invasions. This is based on the large amount of cognate river names found throughout Britain, Ireland and continental Europe which do not seem to be of Celtic origin. They are Indo-European from an earlier time before the various descendant language families – Germanic, Slavonic, Latin, and Celtic – evolved. But accepting this theory doesn't, of course, invalidate the suggestion that there are words, such as those listed above, which do not seem to have Indo-European cognates. Welsh also has a number of similarly unexplained words, pointing to borrowings from an indigenous non-Indo-European language, picked up in Britain, or on the continent (which had, like Welsh, a P-Celtic language, Gaulish) or both. But this, while important to notice, is outwith the scope of the present work.

CHAPTER 9.
CELTIC ON ITS OWN

There are also many instances of Irish/Gaelic words related to Brythonic or even continental Celtic equivalents, which provide instances where both sides of the Celtic family are apparently lacking cognates with the Indo-European languages of Europe. Some examples of both Gaelic and Welsh are:-

Adha – liver. Welsh *afu*.

Banbh – pig(let). This word is now obsolete in Gaelic and Welsh (*banw*) but still in use in Irish. **Muc** is the word normally used today, and it too lacks an Indo-European cognate.

Beul – mouth. There may be a connection with Welsh *gwefl* 'lip', and Irish *béal* is both lip and mouth. An extension of **beul**, in the form **beurla** (earlier *belre*) is an unusual instance of a specific language, English, named after speech-related part, i.e. the mouth, where the language in question is not otherwise specified. This is rather like the Slavonic words for the German language, e.g. *nemetskiy yazyk* in Russian, based on the meaning 'mute' i.e. not speaking Russian, Polish etc. Russian adds the word *yazyk* (language) which Gaelic doesn't, but there is no specific mention of German by name. Like Gaelic, however, Russian has a quite different word for the country Germany – *Germanija* – just as Gaelic uses **Sasann** – Saxon land – for England[19]. The Irish/Gaelic use of *beurla* (mouthings!) for the English language is an early indication the assertive and aggressive presence of English even a millennium ago; it was enough to simply mention 'the speech' for everyone to know who you meant. The Brythonic languages, based in Britain, were far more familiar with the incomers and referred to the English language by name, as Welsh *saesneg*.

---

[19] Other Slavonic languages, however, stick to the 'mute' root, as Polish *Niemcy*.

The Celtic languages are unusual, however, in naming the country of England after the Saxons, while the rest of Europe refers to the Angles. The exception to this is Welsh *Lloegr*, which it is tempting, in this context, to view as a much-mangled form of the Old English variants *Angle*, *Engel* and *Ongel* with metathesis, with the addition of the traditional Welsh suffix *-r* indicating nationality, as *Albanwr* 'a Scot' from *yr Alban* 'Scotland'. But there are difficulties with this.

Broc – badger. Old English *broc* was borrowed from the Celtic. Welsh *broch*. As usual there have been many suggested cognates, the most likely being Greek *phorkos* 'white, grey', since Celtic initial *b* equates to Greek initial *ph*. But again there is no certainty. *Phorkos* is interesting in that it is an example of a word not found in any Greek author, but preserved only in the fifth century AD lexicographer Hesychius, who collected rare words. There are other instances of suggested Gaelic cognates found only in Hesychius.

Calma – brave. Welsh *celfydd* means 'able, competent'.

Ceann – head. The Welsh form is *pen*, which suggested the controversial theory that the Apennines in Italy are from this root, with the meaning of 'top'. This is quite possible since Gaulish, a Celtic language, was spoken in north Italy down to the first century BC and was a P-Celtic language. The Pennines in England, which first appear in print in the 18th century, may have been called after the Apennines, or they may represent another instance of the Welsh *pen*, or rather its Old British or Cumbric version, apparently spoken in the north of England up to the early Middle Ages. Place names tend to preserve old and obsolete words.

Cuid – a part, piece. Welsh *peth* and Pictish *pit*. The English word 'piece', borrowed from Old French, belongs here. French *pièce*, and the forms in other Romance languages derive from a late Latin *pet(t)ia* or similar. The Latin is thought to have been a borrowing from a Celtic language, probably one in continental Europe; Gaulish, being P-Celtic, is a likely candidate. The Pictish *pit(t)*, which appears as *pett* in several instances in the Gaelic notes in the Book of Deer (12th century) means 'a piece of land', and is very common in placenames – around three hundred of them – mostly in the North-East, as Pitlochry. In modern Gaelic *pit* is usually translated as **baile** 'town'. **Cuid** isn't used in this way, unless **Cuidreach** in Skye, of uncertain meaning, is an instance[20].

Fitheach – raven. Welsh *gwyach* is 'a grebe'; Gaelic initial *f* normally becomes *gw* in Welsh. Irish also has *foitheach* 'grebe', which may be a different word from **fitheach**. The two birds are quite unrelated.

Feamainn – seaweed. Welsh *gwymon*.

Gorm – blue, dark blue, green. Welsh *gwrm* can also mean 'brown', and even 'black' (but not 'green'). As this suggests words for colour in the Celtic languages have quite a broad spectrum, and this is a feature of other languages too. The Roman poet Horace describes swans as purple, referring to their brilliant sheen.

Gu lèir – all, together. Welsh *llwyr*.

Lionn – beer. Related to Welsh *llyn* 'lake, (drinkable) water'.

Luch – mouse. Welsh *llygoden*. No convincing Indo-European cognates and the root is restricted to the Celtic languages.

Minidh – awl. Welsh *mynawyd*. A suggested connection with Classical Greek *sminue* 'a hoe' is unlikely, since Indo-European initial *sm-* remains *sm-* in Gadhelic[21].

Reamhar – fat, thick. Welsh *rhef*.

---

[20] Its location may be against this, but there are a couple of Pit- placenames in Glenelg.

[21] It does, in fact, become *m-* in the Brythonic side of the family, which would have suited the Welsh on its own, but all the Celtic languages go together.

Rinn – promontory. Welsh *rhyn*, more usually *penrhyn*.

Sabaid – a fight, row. This word is cited here on the assumption that French *tabut*, with the same meaning, is not from a separate Indo-European root. French dictionaries of Breton think that it may have been borrowed from Breton, but could also be onomatopoeic. An alternative Gaelic form **tabaid**, to which *tabut* may be related, presumably arose from a misunderstanding of **an t-sabaid** 'the fight' where the *s* isn't sounded, as is normal in Gaelic.

Sian – bad weather. Welsh *hin*. Gadhelic initial *s* becomes *h* in the Brythonic languages. Welsh also has the more emphatic *drycin* – i.e. *drwg hin* 'stormy weather'. A similar Gaelic phrase is **sìde nan seachd siantan** referring to seven different types of bad weather – storm, hail etc.

Smeur – bramble. Welsh *miaren*. For the loss of initial *s* in the Welsh, see **minidh** above.

CHAPTER 10.
DIFFERENCES IN MEANING

There are also instances where Irish/Gaelic has words cognate with other Indo-European languages of Europe but which now have a different, or more specific, meaning. There is nothing unusual or surprising about this, of course. Change of meaning is a feature of most languages; English 'nice', for example, is ultimately from a Latin root meaning 'ignorant, simple minded' and the ubiquitous French negatives *pas, point* etc., originally 'a step, point' now simply mean 'not'. The Celtic languages themselves do this a lot; Gaelic **damh** is a 'stag' or 'ox', while the cognate Welsh *dafad* is a 'sheep'. The reason in this instance is that they are both from the same Indo-European root meaning 'tame' – itself an English cognate – and so can be used by various languages to describe (semi)-domesticated animals. Latin *damma* refers to various types of deer, while in Classical Greek *damalis* means 'a young cow'. Stags could hardly be described as tame in Scotland or Ireland (more likely in Scandinavia) but **damh** is thought to be a shortened version of **damh-allaidh** 'wild ox'. Some Indo-European and Gaelic examples of differences in meanings are:-

Bainne – milk. This is from earlier Irish word meaning 'a drop'. There is a Sanskrit cognate, but the word is not used in Modern European languages. In Gaelic today the word for 'a drop' is **boinne**, which is also the Lewis Gaelic for 'milk', which seems appropriate given the origin of **bainne**. But it may be that **boinne** is simply the Lewis pronunciation of **bainne**; Lewis Gaelic often has its own way of sounding vowels.

Banntrach – widow(er). A curious word in that it is the same form for widow and widower, although of course the context and the definite article would clarify matters. But none of the other Celtic languages use exactly the same form of a word for both. The use of **banntrach** for widow is quite understandable since it means a female householder, with **ban** widely used as a female prefix, as **banaltram** 'a nurse', **bànrigh** 'queen' etc., from **bean** 'woman'. The second part of the word was **treabhach**, 'ploughing, farming » farmstead' in Old Irish, and widely found today in the form *tref* in placenames (as is its English cognate *thorp*) and as the Welsh word for 'home'. So the general idea is that the homestead is being run by a woman because her husband has died. But why the same word should also be used of a widower is unclear, and the modern Irish attempt to clarify matters by adding a word meaning 'man' – as *baintreach fir* – seems a bit of an oxymoron.

Only Gaelic, with Irish and Manx, describe a widow(er) in this way. The other half of the Celtic family are different; Welsh *gweddw* is cognate with 'widow', standard Indo-European. Irish in fact also had this root, as *feadhbh*, but it has fallen out of use. Breton, surprisingly, has *intanvez*, based on the numeral 'one', a method used also by Swedish and Danish, as well as Old Irish which used it to mean a single, i.e. unmarried person. You might have expected Breton to follow Welsh, to which it is very closely related, or to have followed French *veuve* (standard Indo-European); French has influenced Breton quite a bit over the centuries. But it's actually nearer to Old Irish.

Drochaid – a bridge. The basis of this word refers to 'tree, oak' – Gaelic **darach** – the most likely etymology. In which case there are cognates in other European language families, but none of these languages uses this as root as their word for 'bridge'.

Eòrna – barley. A possible cognate is English *earn*, which goes back to a Germanic root concerned with the harvest and the income earned from gathering it. Related are the English dialect *earns* 'ears of corn lying on the ground' and *earn* 'to glean'.

Greusaiche – a cobbler. The word's origin is in a Celtic root meaning 'artisan' but only Gaelic uses it in this specialist meaning.

Grian – sun. This word appears only in Gaelic (and Irish and Manx, of course) for 'sun'; all the other European languages of Indo-European origin, without exception use another root meaning 'shine, brightness', of which *sun* is the instance in English, *sol* in Latin and so on. **Grian** is from a different Indo-European root meaning 'heat, warmth', and has a cognate in Sanskrit. What is initially surprising, perhaps, is that the Brythonic (Welsh, Breton, Cornish) half of the Celtic language family go with the rest of Europe, using a word (*haul*) from the same root as 'sun'. Perhaps Gaelic chose **grian** because it used the 'sun, solar' root for the word 'eye', **sùil**, see below. It is significant that none of the other European languages follow Gaelic in this; their words for 'eye' are from different Indo-European roots, none of them related to **sùil**.

Latha – day. There are cognates in Slavonic but these are more general, meaning 'year' or 'summer', not 'day'. But in English 'day' can be used equally vaguely, as 'in my day this was never allowed' with the sense of 'many years ago'. Gaelic has this sense too – **nam latha-sa** – though this is probably a calque (a kind of literal translation).

Làir – mare. This word may be cognate with Greek *polos*, 'foal' – of either sex – and Albanian *pelë* 'mare' has also been suggested. The first *o* in *polos* is long (omega), as is the *à* in **làir**. The loss of Indo-European initial *p* in Irish/Gaelic is the normal development.

Mathan – a bear. A shorter form of earlier Irish *mathghamhain*. The Gaelic is thought to be from **math** 'good', a euphemism to appease a dangerous creature. This would suit **gamhainn** 'a calf' – or another young animal such as deer – quite well also, giving a couthy image of the bear[22]. This was a later use of *mathghamhain*,

---

[22] This sort of thing was not uncommon; the Furies (Erinyes) in Greek mythology were usually referred to as Eumenides (kind people), and in Gaelic, *aingeal* 'angel' was used by fishermen, for instance, to avoid saying *teine* 'fire', a potentially dangerous thing. This may also explain *tuath* 'north' if it is cognate with Latin *tutus* 'safe, in good hands' since the original meaning of *tuath* was 'left (handed), unlucky', a meaning found now in *tuathal* 'unlucky, awkward'.

since the earlier Irish word for bear was *art*, as is still the case in Brythonic Celtic, e.g. Welsh *arth*; though not too much later, as the brown bear is thought to have been extinct in Ireland before the first millennium BC. The Celtic *art* was very likely the original Indo-European root, since it is found today in the Romance languages (from Latin *artus*); the Slavonic languages call the bear by a word meaning 'honey eater', while the Germanic 'bear' is cognate with 'brown'.

Reithe – a ram. This word is related to **ruith** 'to run' and so the ram is apparently 'the runner'. The Indo-European cognate is Latin *rota* 'wheel', English 'rotate', and so on in the Germanic and Romance languages.

Tric – often. Thought to be from an Indo-European root meaning 'to run, rush' a sense seen more clearly in Irish, where it can also mean 'quick, hasty'.

There are also Irish/Gaelic words with Brythonic or even continental Celtic cognates, which have Indo-European cognates with a different meaning from the Celtic. Some examples are:-

Beag – small. Welsh *bach*. Cognates have been suggested with Sanskrit and Armenian from an Indo-European root *b^heg meaning 'to break', the idea being 'broken into pieces', i.e. small. A nasalised form of the root (see introduction) gives English 'bang' i.e. to hammer. **Bochd** 'poor' may be from the same root; compare colloquial English 'broke', i.e. penniless.

Ciad – first. Cognate with Latin *recent*, i.e. new, and Greek *kainos* 'new' found in erudite English scientific terms as *kainite*, a white mineral, *eocene*, a geological epoch, etc. Gaelic agrees with the other Indo-European languages in having no connection etymologically between 'first' and the numeral 'one'. Welsh *cyntaf*.

Cnoc – hill. The Germanic cognate is seen in English 'neck', which was earlier *hnekka*. Gaelic initial *c* for English initial *h* is a standard Indo-European development. The meaning of the Indo-

European root is 'lump, projection' as in the 'neck' of a bottle. In modern Welsh *cnwch* means a 'hump, protuberance', but is no longer used of hills.

Cuileag – a fly. The Latin cognate, *culex*, is a midge or gnat. But Gaelic has **meanbh-chuileag** 'a small fly' for a midge. Welsh *cylion*.

Ear – east. The cardinal points of the compass in Gaelic are indirectly related to Indo-European roots. **Ear** 'east' is based on a root meaning 'before, against, in front of' and refers to the Irish arrangement of facing east with the rising sun in front of you. **Iar** 'west' is based on another root with the meaning 'behind'. **Tuath** 'north', mentioned above in a footnote to **mathan**, is probably a euphemism for left (handed) which was considered unlucky; a common word for left-handed, **ceàrr**, has 'wrong' as its primary meaning. **Deas** 'south' refers to the right hand (side) as you face east, based on a common Indo-European root of which English 'dextrous' is an example. Irish/Gaelic has the only instances of these roots used to describe the four points of the compass, with the exception of Welsh, which concurs with Gaelic in its word for south, *de*. Other Indo-European languages of Europe have references to rising, setting, left and the sun, and most of them use the same system of facing east to assign the compass points. A notable exception is Classical Greek where points of the compass were based on facing north. So *skaios*, one of the words for 'left (side)' also meant 'west'. Homer's *Iliad* is full of references to the *Skaian*, i.e. western, gate of Troy.

Gaelic/Irish stands alone, however, in its treatment of the ordinal – also known as intercardinal – points of the compass. It reverses the word order found in all the other Indo-European language families so that 'south-west' for instance, is **iar-dheas**, which translates literally as 'west-south'. Similarly, 'north-east' is **ear-thuath** (east-north) and so on. This seems to reflect the fact that the east was the starting, and therefore the most important, point for describing directions in Irish, and so is the leading member of the compound. West was similarly treated by analogy. The Brythonic Celtic languages don't follow Gaelic in this, so Gaelic may have adopted this unusual arrangement after the division of the Celtic language family into Gadhelic and Brythonic. It certainly predates the beginning of the influence of English on Gaelic; nowadays adjectival combinations such as 'black and white' (photographs etc.) are 'white and black' in Italian and Spanish for instance (*bianco nero*), but Gaelic will follow the English – so **dubh is geal**.

Laogh – calf. The probable cognates in Latvian and Albanian refer to 'cow' or 'cattle' and have the Indo-European *p* which is missing in Gaelic, as normal. Welsh *llo*.

Luaithre, luath – ashes. There are cognates in Greek, Latin and Germanic but they have the meaning 'wash'. The Gaelic has developed from the Germanic, seen in English 'lye', a washing agent made by adding ashes to water. The nearest Gaelic word for this, **buaic**, and words for 'lather' (**cop**) and 'soap' (**siabann**) are all borrowed from English and have no etymological connection with **luaithre**. Welsh *lludw*.

Saor – joiner, carpenter. This has cognates in the Romances languages with the general idea of knowledge, skill, craftsmanship, but is now restricted to 'carpenter' in Gaelic. Rather surprisingly the modern Celtic languages have not used their native root found in the word 'carpenter', which English borrowed from French (it's also in Spanish), which in turn had borrowed it from Latin *carpentarius*. This goes back to the P-Celtic Gaulish word *carpentum* 'chariot, two-wheeled vehicle' borrowed by the Romans. It survives in modern Gaelic as **carbad** 'chariot, vehicle, car', and Welsh *cerbyd*. Welsh *saer*.

Sùil – eye. All the Indo-European cognates of this word (Germanic, Romance, Slavonic etc.) refer to the sun, not to the human eye. For Gaelic, however, the sun is the eye in the sky, an idea found in other languages such as Indonesian, Malay etc. Mata

Hari, a Dutch woman who spied for Germany during the first world war, had lived for a time in Indonesia, then a Dutch colony, and used this as a stage name, meaning the 'eye of the day (or dawn)'. An appropriate name for a spy! As mentioned above, Gaelic uses a different word, **grian**, for 'sun'. For Welsh *haul* 'sun', cognate with **sùil**, see also under **grian**. Welsh initial *h*- from Indo-European initial *s*- is a feature which it shares with Greek, and, indirectly, with English words such as helium and the several helio- compounds, meaning 'sun', borrowed from Greek.

CPSIA information can be obtained
at www.ICGtesting.com
Printed in the USA
LVHW080115300422
717544LV00019B/998